Circle ○ the coins that **equal 4¢**.

Draw a line to match each **letter pair**.

G	h
H	i
I	a
A	g

Draw a line from each number to its matching set.

Write the letter that comes **next**.

A

B

A

B

A

____

Draw a line to match the pictures that **rhyme**.

Circle ○ the boy who looks **happy**.

Circle ◯ what you would wear.

Circle ◯ the person who is **first** in line.

Circle ◯ the picture that shows **why** this happened.

Circle ◯ the **beginning** letter.

p r

d j

Circle ◯ the word that **goes with** the picture.

dad dog did

Write how many there are **in all**.

2 + 2 = ___

Circle ◯ the group that has **fewer** cars.

Write the missing number.

5 6 ___ 8 9

15 16 ___ 18 19

Color to finish the **pattern**.

Color to finish the **pattern**.

Number the pictures in **1**, **2**, **3** order to show what happens **first**, **next**, and **last**.

Draw a line to match each **letter pair**.

M	n
N	c
O	m
C	o

Draw a line to match the pictures that **rhyme**.

Write the number that comes **next**.

1

2

1

2

1

____

Circle ◯ the group that has **more** ladybugs.

Write the number that comes **before**.

___ 8 9

___ 15 16

Circle ◯ the **amount**.

10¢ 15¢ 9¢

Circle ◯ the letters that are in **a b c** order.

a b c d

a d b c

Count by **2**'s.
Write the missing number.

2 4 6 ___ 10

12 14 ___ 18 20

Circle ◯ the mouse on **top**.

Draw a line to match the **opposites**.

loud

full

up

down

empty

quiet

the shape that does **not belong**.
Color.

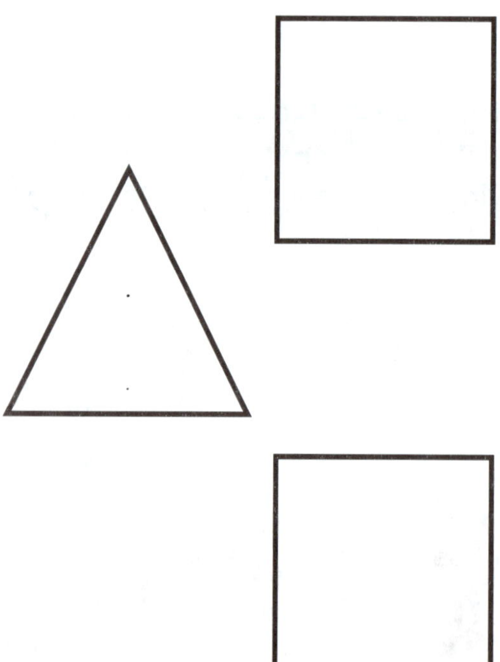

the flower that is **taller**.
Circle the flower that is **shorter**.

Circle ○ the dog that is **inside**.

Circle ○ the **action** word.

walk run sit

Circle ○ the **ending** letter.

x d

c b

Write how many there are **in all**.

3 + 3 = ____

Color the picture.

1 = red 2 = blue 3 = green 4 = yellow 5 = purple

✓ the kite with the **longest** tail.

Draw a line to match the pictures that **rhyme**.

Number the pictures in **1**, **2**, **3** order to show what happens **first**, **next**, and **last**.

___ ___ ___

Draw a line to show who uses each object.

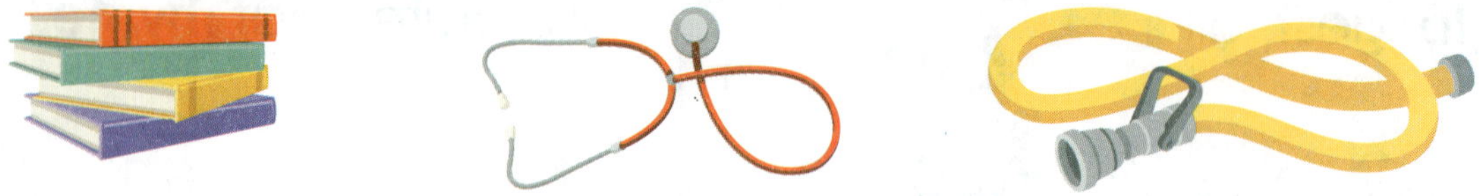

Trace the **square**.
How many sides does it have? **2 3 4**

Circle ◯ the word that means the **opposite** of **dry**.

big wet nice

Circle ◯ the word that means the **opposite** of **hot**.

cold low new

Write how many  there are **in all**.

$$3 + 2 = \_\_\_$$

Circle the vegetables.
the fruit.

Draw a line to match each **letter pair**.

U v

V e

W u

E w

Circle how many **parts** of the word you hear.

bird 1 2

apple 1 2

balloon 1 2

Circle what you would wear.

Draw a line to where the frog lives.

Draw a line to match the **opposites**.

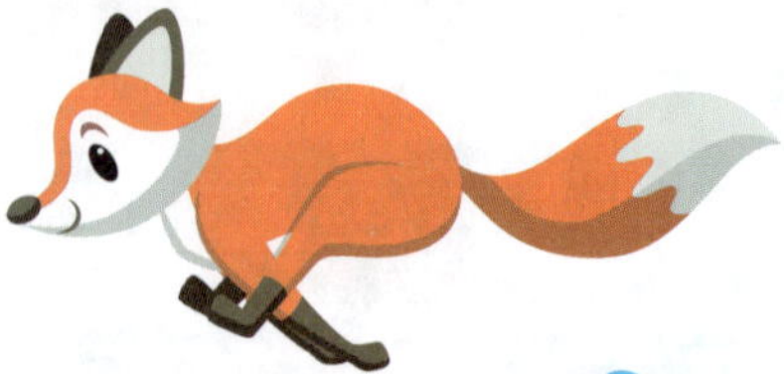

fast

right

stop

slow

left

go

Circle ◯ the **beginning** letter.

d b

l c

Circle ◯ the word that **names** the picture.

big pig pat

Circle ◯ where you can shop for a dog.

Circle ◯ the clock that shows **4:00**.

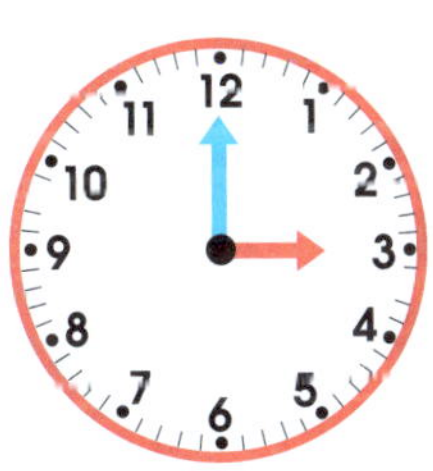

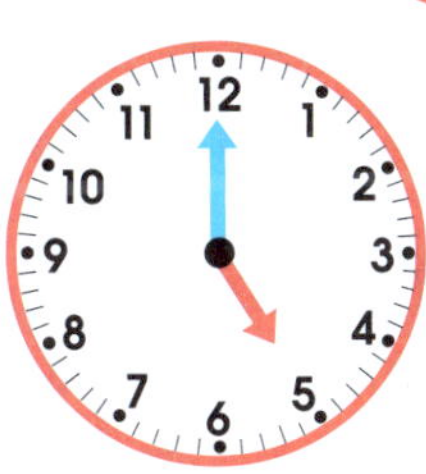

Write the letter that comes **before**.

___ c d e

___ k l m

the group that has **fewer** frogs.

Circle the **amount**.

7¢ 9¢ 8¢

Circle the group with a **greater** number of fish.

Circle the **action** word.

hop fly run

Circle the letters that are in **a b c** order.

d f g h

d e f g

Circle the **ending** letter.

p r

l n

Draw and color the shape that comes **next**.

Circle everything that is alive.

Draw a line to match the pictures that **rhyme**.

Write how many snails there are **in all**.

4 + 2 = ____

Circle the **beginning** letter.

h f

h k

Write the number that is **between**.

10 ___ 12

17 ___ 19

✗ the snake that is the **longest**.
✓ the snake that is the **shortest**.

Number the pictures in **1**, **2**, **3** order to show what happens **first**, **next**, and **last**.

______ ______ ______

❌ the shape that does **not belong**.

Color.

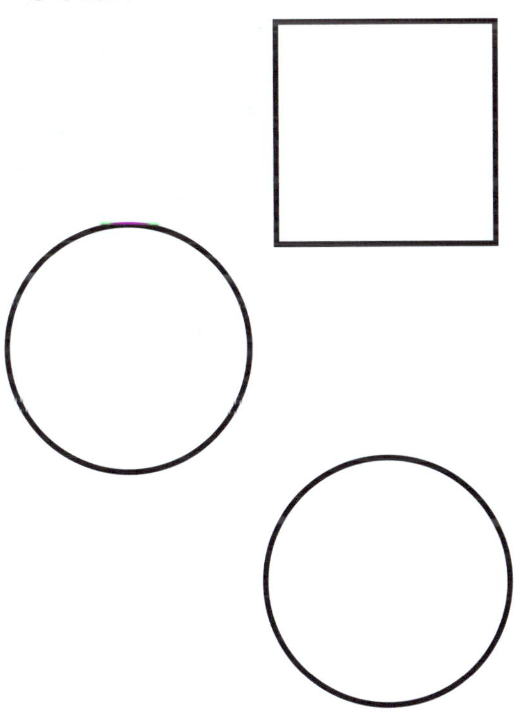

Draw a line to match each **letter pair**.

J	j
K	l
L	b
B	k

Find and circle ◯ the hidden pictures.

Color the balloon to finish the **pattern**.

Draw a line to match the mitten pairs.
Which mitten does **not** have a match? Circle ○ it.

Circle ○ the coin that is worth the **most**.

Circle ○ the clock that shows **3:00**.

Circle ○ the number that is **1 more** than **6**.

7 4 5

Circle ○ the number that is **1 less** than **6**.

4 5 3

Count by **5**'s.
Write the missing numbers.

5 10 __ 20 25

10 15 __ 25 30

Circle ○ the bag that holds **more**.

Circle ○ the day that comes **after** Sunday.

Saturday

Friday

Monday

Write how many are left.

5 − 2 = ___

Trace the **triangle**.
How many sides does it have? **3 4 5**

Circle ○ what is **heavier**.

Draw the missing apples to show **6**.
Color.

Circle ◯ the letters that are in **a b c** order.

p n o r

m n o p

Circle ◯ the action word.

fly run hop

Write how many are left.

8 − 3 = ___

Circle ◯ the clock that shows **8:00**.

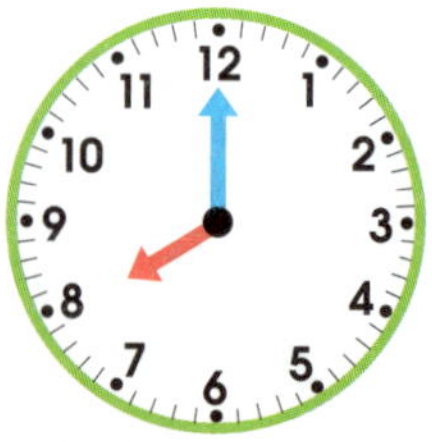

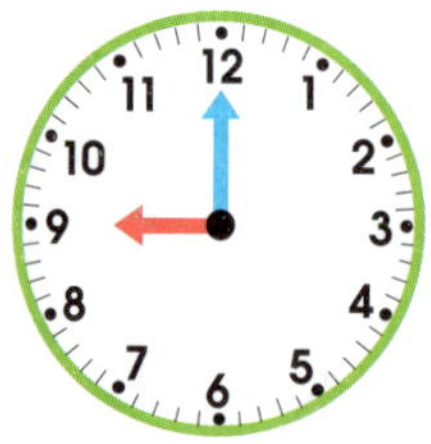

Circle ◯ the **ending** letter.

t i

s g

Draw a line to match the **opposites**.

wet

above

below

back

front

dry

Number the pictures in **1**, **2**, **3** order to show what happens **first**, **next**, and **last**.

_____ _____ _____

Draw a line to match each **letter pair**.

S	p
X	x
R	s
P	r

Draw a line to match the pictures that **rhyme**.

Draw the picture that comes **next**.

Write the missing letter.

g h ___ j k l

u v w ___ y z

Write the number that comes **after**.

1 2 3 ___

8 9 10 ___

Write how many  **are left.**

5 – 1 = ___

Circle ◯ the word that **names** the picture.

big bad bug

Circle ◯ the **beginning** letter.

r w

z n

Number the pictures in **1**, **2**, **3** order to show what happens **first**, **next**, and **last**.

✗ the shape that does **not belong**.
Color.

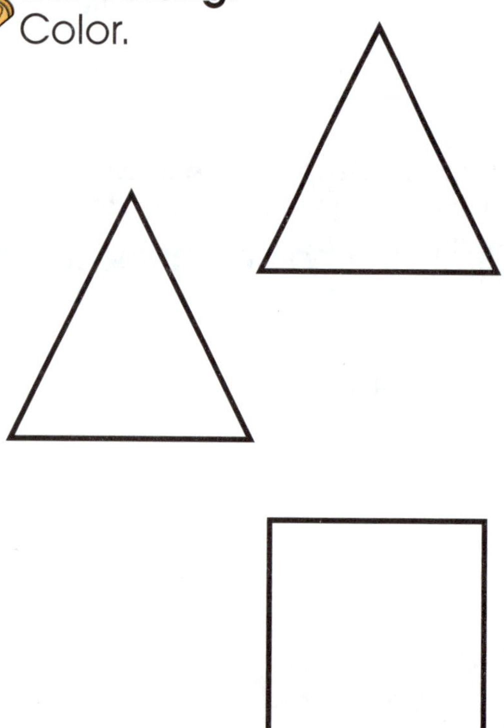

✓ the picture that shows $\frac{1}{2}$.

Draw the missing yo-yos to show **4**.
Color.

Circle ◯ the **ending** letter.

k d

f j

Write the letter that comes **after**.

m n o ___

c d e ___

Write how many  **are left**.

$5 - 2 = $ ___

Connect the dots from **1** to **25**.
Color the picture.

Draw a line to match the pictures that **rhyme**.

Circle ◯ the animal that gives us milk.

Circle ◯ the boy in the **middle**.

Circle ○ the coins that **equal 7¢**.

Circle ○ **2** words that are the **same**.

mat cat

cow

cat sat

Circle ○ **2** things you need to wash your dog.

Draw a line to match each **letter pair**.

F	z
T	t
D	f
Z	d

Draw a line to match the pictures that **rhyme**.

Jane spent **8¢**. What did she buy?

Write the **beginning** letter.

___ug

___ox

Draw a line from each item to the correct recycling bin.

Match each word to the picture.

ball 

balls 

duck 

ducks 

book 

books 

Fill in the missing number.

10 9 8 ___ 6

4 3 2 ___ 0

8 7 6 ___ 4

Circle ◯ the girl who looks **sad**.

Match the **amounts**.

9¢

7¢

5¢

Circle ◯ the person who is **last** in line.

Circle ◯ the picture that shows **why** this happened.

Circle ○ the item that costs the **most**.

Circle ○ **2** things you need to play baseball.

Circle ○ the things that are alive.

Circle ○ the **slower** animal.

Circle ○ the picture that has the **long a** sound in **rake**.

Circle ◯ the one that does **not belong**.

fast

hot

Number the pictures in **1**, **2**, **3** order to show what happens **first**, **next**, and **last**.

Draw a line to match the pictures that have the same **short vowel** sound.

Circle ○ the pictures that begin with the **tr sound**.

Draw a line to match the same times.

5:00

3:00

8:00

9:00

Circle ○ the one that weighs **less**.

Circle ○ the pictures that **rhyme**.

Circle ○ the shapes that have **equal** parts.

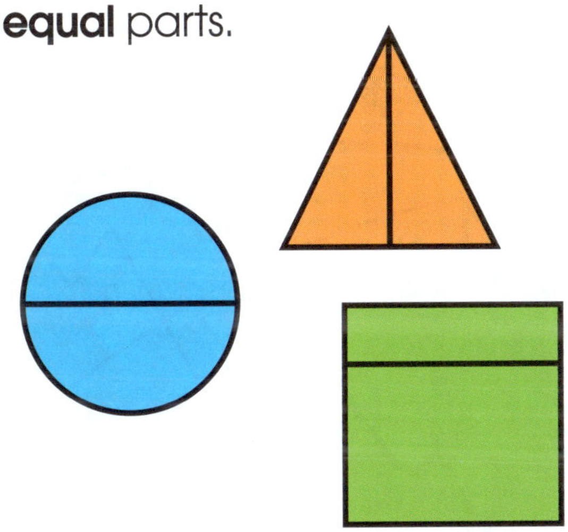

Circle ○ the one that is **smaller**.

Circle ○ the word that **names** the picture.

run sun bug

Write the **beginning** letter.

____at

Color the picture.

1 = red 2 = blue 3 = green 4 = orange 5 = brown

Draw a line to match the color words to the colors.

red

yellow

blue

orange

Circle ○ the things you can hear.

Circle ○ the shape that does **not belong**.

Draw the missing balloons to match the number.

10

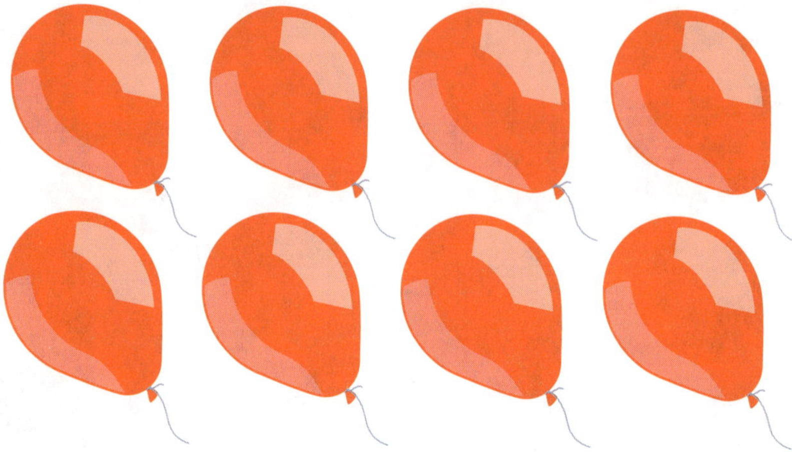

Circle ○ the picture that has the **long e** sound.

Write the **ending** letter.

moo___

pi___

Draw an X on what does **not belong**.

When does this happen?

night morning

Number the pictures in **a b c** order.

Number the pictures in **1**, **2**, **3** order to show what happens **first**, **next**, and **last**.

Circle ○ what happened **before**.

Circle ○ the one that is alive.

Circle ○ the picture that has the **long i** sound in **bike**.

Circle ○ what happens **next**.

I grow on trees. Monkeys love me. What am I?

I have four legs. I have a hard shell. What am I?

Which dog is the **same size**?

Which one takes people to the hospital?

Circle what you would wear.

Draw a line to where each animal lives.

land

water

Match each number to the pictures.

11 

12 

13 

14 

15 

Circle the picture that begins with the letter **d**.

Circle the house on the **right**.

Write how many there are **in all**.

$3 + 2 =$ ____

Circle the **oldest** person.

Circle the word that **names** the picture.

dish cow fish

Circle ◯ the one that is **longer**.

Draw an **X** on the word that is **different**.

did

dog dog

cat can

cat

Circle ◯ the star that is **outside**.

Write the **beginning** letter.

___aw

___ox

Circle ◯ the picture that has the **long o** sound as in **boat**.

Circle ◯ the **name** of the shape.

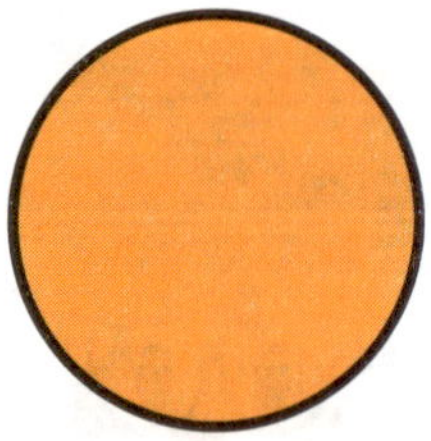

circle

square triangle

Circle ◯ the shape that comes **next**.

Draw lines to the mittens that are the **same size**.

Circle ◯ the coins that **equal 14¢**.

Find and circle ◯ the hidden pictures.

Write the missing number.

 + ___ = 

6 + ___ = 7

Is the bird **on** or **off** the birdhouse?

on off

Circle the word that **names** the picture.

bat boy ball

Look at the graph.
Answer the questions.

How **many** [chocolate]? ______ How **many** [strawberry]? ______

Write the number that comes **before**.

___ 8 9   ___ 14 15   ___ 12 13

Write the number that comes **between**.

10 ___ 12   9 ___ 11   18 ___ 20

Write the number that comes **after**.

7 8 ___   13 14 ___   17 18 ___

Circle ◯ the one that is the **shortest**.

Circle ◯ how many **parts** of the word you hear.

elephant 1 2 3

cow 1 2 3

teapot 1 2 3

Circle ◯ the toy that is **below** the truck.

Match each word to the picture.

hat ten pig mop sun

Write the missing **ending** letter.

we___

an___

Circle ◯ **2** words that are the **same**.

big by

but

can big

Circle ◯ the number that is **1 more** than **9**.

8 12 10

Circle ◯ the number that is **1 more** than **19**.

20 18 15

Circle ◯ the **name** of the shape.

circle

square triangle

Circle ◯ the dog that is **off**.

Circle ◯ what is white and has feathers.

Underline the sentence that **goes with** the picture.

It is jumping over.

It is jumping under.

Draw a **square** using the dots.

Circle the one that is **empty**.

Draw the missing strawberries to show **12**.

Draw an X on what is **make-believe**.

Circle ○ the picture that begins with the **sh sound** in **shoe**.

Circle ○ the picture that shows **why** this happened.

Write the **ending** letter.

bu____

Circle ○ the cat on **top**.

Draw a line to match each word to a picture.

over

under

inside

outside

Number the pictures in **1**, **2**, **3** order to show what happens **first**, **next**, and **last**.

Match the pictures that have the same **long vowel** sound.

Circle ○ the **action** word.

run

jump walk

Write the number that comes **next**.

5

4

3

5

4

____

Write the **beginning** letter.

___eb

Circle ○ the number that is **1 less** than **9**.

12 8 10

Circle ○ the number that is **1 less** than **12**.

10 9 11

Circle ○ the pizza that covers the most **area**.

When does this happen?

morning night

Circle ○ the **name** of the shape.

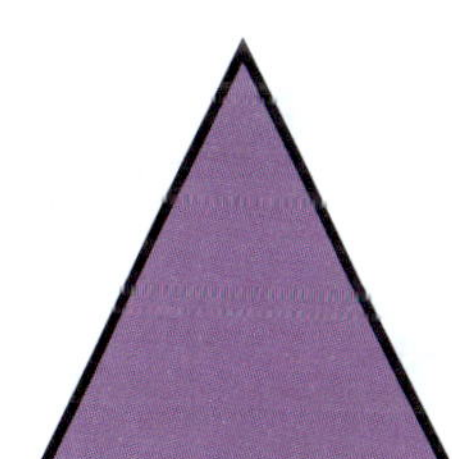

circle

square triangle

Connect the dots from **1** to **25**.
Color the picture.

Solve the problem.

$$6 + 4 = \underline{\qquad}$$

Circle ◯ the ball that bounced the **highest**.

Color $\frac{1}{2}$ of the triangle.

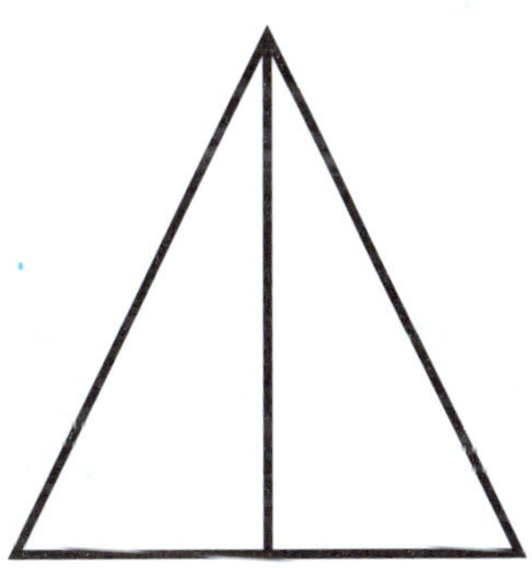

Color $\frac{1}{2}$ of the circle.

Circle ○ the toy that is **next to** the lion.

Circle ○ the triangle that is **outside**.

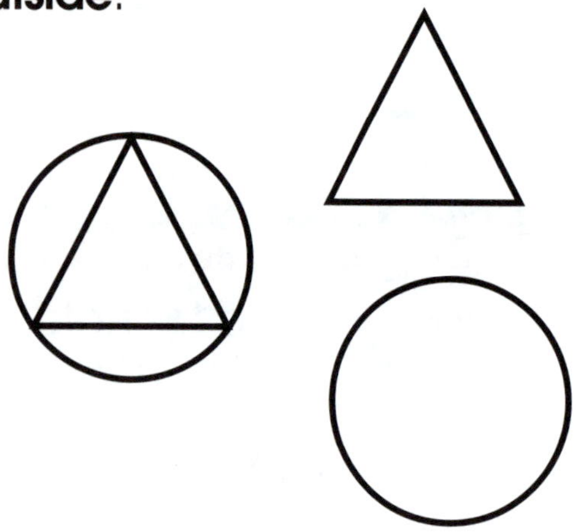

What time of year is it?

summer winter

Draw lines to match the clocks that show the **same** time.

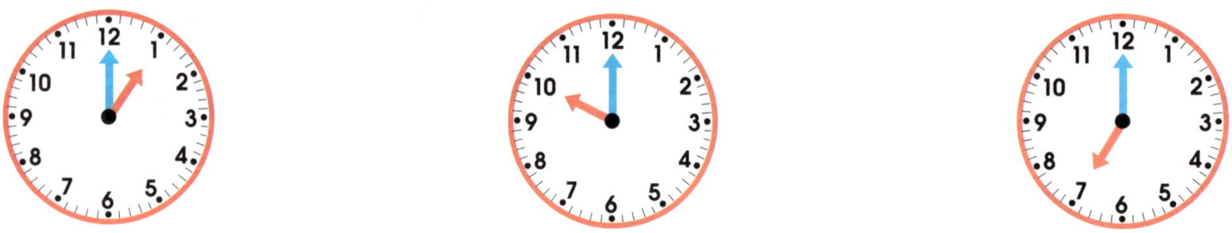

Circle ○ the action that takes **less time**.

Circle ○ the animal that gives us eggs.

Circle ○ the line that is **longer**.

Count by **10**'s.
Circle ○ the **amount**.

10¢ 20¢ 30¢

Circle ○ **2** words that are the **same**.

six see

stop

see saw

Circle ○ **2** things you need to brush your teeth.

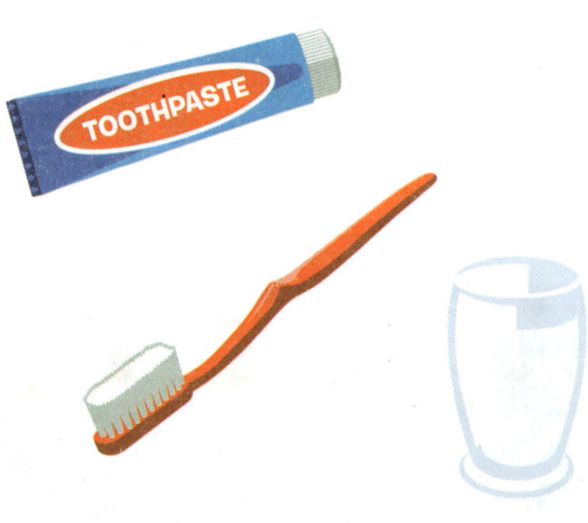

Match the pictures that have the same **beginning sound**.

Circle ○ the picture that weighs the **most**.